Melbourne has something for everyone, which is probably part of the reason why it regularly tops lists as the world's most livable city. Besides a thriving arts community, a leading fashion industry, and a skyline that blends cutting-edge contemporary architecture with historical buildings that are all intertwined at street level by a system of alleyways housing some of the world's best street art, it is also home to a burgeoning restaurant, café, and bar scene.

CITIx60: Melbourne explores Australia's cultural and arts capital in five aspects, covering architecture, art spaces, shopping, dining and entertainment. With expert advice from 60 stars of the local creative scene, this book guides you to the real attractions of the city for an authentic taste of Melbourne life.

Contents

Before You Go

BASIC INFO

Currency
Australian Dollar (AUD/$)
Exchange rate: US$1 : A$1.4

Time zone
GMT +10
DST +1*

*DST begins at 0200 (local time) on the first Sunday of October and ends at 0300 (local time) on the first Sunday of April.

Dialling
International calling: +61
Citywide: (0)3*

*Dial (0) for calls made within Australia.

Weather (avg. temperature range)
Spring (Sep-Nov): 10-22°C / 50-72°F
Summer (Dec-Feb): 13-25°C / 55-77°F
Autumn (Mar-May): 9-20°C / 48-68°F
Winter (Jun-Aug): 6-13°C / 43-55°F

USEFUL WEBSITES

Public transport info & timetables
www.ptv.vic.gov.au

Free public WiFi hotspot locator
www.visitvictoria.com/Information/WiFi-hotspots

EMERGENCY CALLS

Ambulance, fire or police
000

Consulates
China	+61 (0)3 9822 0604
France	+61 (0)3 9690 6075
Germany	+61 (0)3 9642 8088
Japan	+61 (0)3 9679 4510
Spain	+61 (0)3 9347 1966
UK	+61 (0)3 9652 1600
US	+61 (0)3 9526 5900

AIRPORT EXPRESS TRANSFERS

Tullamarine Airport <-> Southern Cross Station (SkyBus)
Buses / Journey: Every 10 mins / 20-35 mins depending on traffic
From Tullamarine Airport (T3) ~ 0010-2355
From Southern Cross Station ~ 0005-2355
One-way: $18.75 / Return: $36*
www.skybus.com.au

Avalon Airport <-> Southern Cross Station (SkyBus)
Buses / Journey: Every major flight / ~50 mins
One-way: $24 / Return: $46*
www.skybus.com.au

*Purchase tickets via SkyBus website for discounted fares to apply.

PUBLIC TRANSPORT IN MELBOURNE

Bicycle
Bus
Taxi
Train
Tram

Means of payment
Credit card
Cash
myki pass

GENERAL PUBLIC HOLIDAYS

January	1 New Year's Day, 26 Australia Day
Mar/Apr	Labour Day, Good Friday, Saturday before Easter Sunday, Easter Sunday & Monday, 25 ANZAC Day
June	10 Queen's Birthday
Sept/Oct	Friday before the AFL Grand Final
November	Melbourne Cup
December	25 Christmas Day, 26 Boxing Day

*Museums and galleries are normally open on public holidays, except during Good Friday and Christmas.

FESTIVALS / EVENTS

February
White Night Melbourne (or August)
whitenightmelbourne.com.au
St. Jerome's Laneway Festival
melbourne.lanewayfestival.com

March
Virgin Australia Melbourne Fashion Festival
www.vamff.com.au
Melbourne Art Book Fair
www.ngv.vic.gov.au/whats-on/programs-
events/art-book-fair
Melbourne Design Week
www.ngv.vic.gov.au/melbourne-design-week
Melbourne Food & Wine Festival
www.melbournefoodandwine.com.au

May
Next Wave Biannual Festival
nextwave.org.au

June
Melbourne International Jazz Festival
www.melbournejazz.com
Melbourne Art Fair (or August)
melbourneartfair.com.au

July
Open House Melbourne
www.openhousemelbourne.org

August
Melbourne International Film Festival
(through to September)
miff.com.au

September
Melbourne Fringe Festival
www.melbournefringe.com.au

October
Melbourne International Arts Festival
www.festival.melbourne

Event days vary by year. Please check for
updates online.

UNUSUAL OUTINGS

Melbourne Street Art Tours
www.melbournestreettours.com

Hot Air Balloon Ride
www.balloonman.com.au

Rapjumping
rapjumping.com

Great Ocean Road Tour
greatoceanroadmelbournetours.com.au

The Old Melbourne Gaol Night Tour
www.oldmelbournegaol.com.au

SMARTPHONE APPS

Journey planner
Public Transport Victoria

Bike-sharing
Melbourne Bike-Share

F&B reviews by locals
Zomato

REGULAR EXPENSES

A cappuccino
~$4

Brunch for one
$15–25

Gratuities
Tipping is discretionary in Australia.
Restaurants and bars: 10% of the total bill
For licensed taxis: Round up to the nearest
dollar.

Count to 10

What makes Melbourne so special?

Illustrations by Guillaume Kashima aka Funny Fun

Melbourne is made up of a vibrant and culturally diverse blend of festivals, cuisines, and music. This is a city overflowing with artistic and creative thinkers who express themselves in every facet of everyday life. Whether you are on a one-day stopover or a week-long stay, see what Melbourne's creatives consider essential to see, taste, read, and take home from your trip.

1

Architecture

**Domed Building,
State Library of Victoria**
by Bates, Pebbles & Smart

Cairo Flats
by Acheson Best Overend

Arts Centre Melbourne Spire
by Roy Grounds

Manchester Unity Building (#6)
by Marcus R. Barlow

Burnham Beeches
by Harry A. Norris

Olympic Swimming Stadium
by Kevin Borland, Peter McIntyre,
J & P Murphy

Shrine of Remembrance
updated by Ashton Raggatt
McDougall, Rush Wright & Associates

2

Markets

Handmade designs & fashion
Rose St. Artist Market
www.rosestmarket.com.au

Second-hand & retro goods, antiques
Chapel St. Bazaar
FB: @ChapelStreetBazaar

New & used goods & crafts
Coburg Trash & Treasure
www.trashandtreasure.com.au

Local produce & craft beers
Collingwood Farmers Market
www.vicfarmersmarkets.org.au

Indie art & design
The Finders Keepers
www.thefinderskeepers.com

3

Bookstores

Old & new culinary books
Books for Cooks
www.booksforcooks.com.au

Magazines, books & stationery
Mag Nation
www.magnation.com

Comprehensive art book range
Metropolis @Curtin House
metropolisbookshop.com.au

Small press publications
Perimeter Books
perimeterbooks.com

After-dinner reading spot
The Paperback Bookshop
www.paperbackbooks.com.au

Underground zines, films & comix
Polyester Books
www.polyester.com.au

4

Homegrown Magazines

Broadsheet Melbourne
www.broadsheet.com.au

ACCLAIM
www.acclaimmag.com

FRANKIE
www.frankie.com.au

Process Journal
www.madepublishers.com

Offscreen
www.offscreenmag.com

Archer
archermagazine.com.au

Smith Journal
www.smithjournal.com.au

5

Specialty Coffee Houses & Roasters

NOLA Iced Coffee
Everyday Coffee
www.everyday-coffee.com

Standing room café in a subway
Cup Of Truth
cupoftruth.com.au

'Magic' coffee
Dukes Coffee Roasters
www.dukescoffee.com.au

Coffee, music & design
Brother Baba Budan
IG: @brotherbababudan

Coffee house in an old converted horse stable
Vertue Coffee Roasters
vertuecoffee.com.au

Coffee roastery & retailer
Market Lane
marketlane.com.au

6

Breakfast & Brunch Spots

Japanese-inspired food in a backstreet warehouse
Cibi Café
cibi.com.au

Beautifully crafted brunch
Top Paddock Café
toppaddockcafe.com

Quaint little café
Twenty & Six
www.twentyandsix.com.au

Thai fusion
Magic Mountain Saloon
magicmountainsaloon.com.au

Seasonal breakfast in a beautiful warehouse
East Elevation
eastelevation.com.au

Bircher muesli with dehydrated mandarin
Wide Open Road
wideopenroad.com.au

7

Pastries

Pork roll
N.Lee Bakery
220 Smith St., Collingwood

Salted caramel doughnut
Cobb Lane
www.cobblane.com.au

Doughnuts filled with hot jam
Footscray Doughnuts & Coffee
Footscray train station

Custard doughnuts
Baker D. Chirico
bakerdchirico.com.au

Cheese pies
A1 Bakery
643-645 Sydney Rd., Brunswick

Waffles & baguettes
Waffle On
Shop 9, Degraves St., CBD

8

Street Art Hunting

Original Banksy art
Revolver Upstairs
revolverupstairs.com.au

Hosier & Rutledge Lane
opposite Federation Square

Caledonian Lane
off Little Bourke St.

Union Lane
off Bourke Street Mall

Flinders Lane
corner of Cocker Alley

Carlton
Palmerston St.

Centre Place
between Collins St. &
Flinders Ln.

ACDC Lane
between Exhibition St. &
Russell St.

9

Rooftop Bars

Naked in the Sky
www.nakedforsatan.com.au/
in-the-sky

Bomba (#50)
www.bombabar.com.au

Siglo
siglobar.com.au

Madame Brussels
www.madamebrussels.com

Wolf's Lair & Treetops
jimmywatsons.com/wolfslair

Rooftop Bar @Curtain House (#22)
(Seasonal)
rooftopcinema.com.au

Goldilocks
www.goldilocksbar.com

Loop Roof
www.looprooftopbar.com.au

10

Live Music & Gig Venues

Some Velvet Morning (#57)
somevelvetmorning.com.au

The Standard Hotel in Fitzroy
www.thestandardhotel.com.au

The Retreat in Brunswick
retreathotelbrunswick.com.au

The Spotted Mallard
www.spottedmallard.com

The Corner Hotel
cornerhotel.com

Forum Melbourne (#7)
forummelbourne.com.au

The Toff in Town (#60)
www.thetoffintown.com

Icon Index

 Opening hours   Admission

 Address   Facebook

 Contact   Instagram

Remarks   Website

 Scan QR codes to access Google Maps and discover the area around each destination. Internet connection required.

60x60

60 Local Creatives x 60 Hotspots

From the city's street art-filled laneways to its wealth of cuisines from all corners of the world, there is much inspiration to be found in Melbourne. 60x60 points you to 60 haunts where 60 arbiters of taste find theirs.

Landmarks & Architecture
SPOTS · 01 – 12

Marvel at the seamless blend of contemporary structures, graffiti-clad laneways, and green open spaces. Start at Federation Square and meander through to Melbourne University.

Cultural & Art Spaces
SPOTS · 13 – 24

Be spoilt for choice with theatre, comedy, dance, ballet, musicals, indigenous crafts, sculptures, classical or contemporary art and much more happening every day.

Markets & Shops
SPOTS · 25 – 36

Get lost trawling through unique souvenir stores, charming boutiques, earth-friendly markets, high-end fashion stores, craft-focused spaces, and everything in between.

Restaurants & Cafés
SPOTS · 37 – 48

Start your day with a hearty breakfast or brunch, stop for a coffee break at an artisanal roastery, and take in stunning sunset views with a cocktail in hand from a rooftop bar.

Nightlife
SPOTS · 49 – 60

Indulge in craft beers, wine, and late-night bites at one of the many eateries and watering holes around the city before catching a live performance or dancing into the wee hours.

Landmarks & Architecture

Historic architecture, cultural precincts, and a sports superstage

The architecture of Melbourne is a beautiful blend of contemporary buildings, open public spaces, abstract architecture (#3), and old Neo-Gothic buildings (#6) – often with street art-filled laneways weaving around them. While North Melbourne's many perfectly maintained Victorian buildings provide a glimpse into the city's elegant past, a walk along the Yarra River through the ritzy suburbs of Toorak, South Yarra, and Hawthorn will reveal some of the most amazing Tudor, Tudorbethan, Georgian, and Victorian mansions built following Melbourne's gold rush during the mid-1800s. To the north of the gridded CBD area, you will find a snapshot of Melbourne's industrial past. When the inner city suburbs of Fitzroy, Collingwood, and Abbotsford were gentrified in the 1980s and 1990s, the surge in rent prices forced out much of the manufacturing industries but magnetised a band of hipsters to re-energise and rejuvenate the abandoned warehouses with creative revival projects. Melbourne's cityscape is also well-balanced by many neatly manicured gardens and huge green parks, such as The Royal Botanic Gardens (*www.rbg.vic.gov.au*), and sportsgrounds such as the MCG (#4), Rod Laver Arena (where the annual Australian Open is played), and AAMI Park. With a relatively flat terrain, the city is best explored by bike or its famously convenient trams. Otherwise, head up to the Edge (*www.eurekaskydeck.com.au*) for breathtaking panoramas. The four-sided glass cube commands all-encompassing views from Melbourne's tallest building, the Eureka Tower in Southbank.

Studio Constantine
Communication design studio

We are Hannah and David Constantine of Studio Constantine. Everything we do and make is committed to being beautiful, articulate, incisive, and relevant to our clients and their markets.

University of Melbourne P.016

Archier
Design studio

Composed of architects Chris Haddad, Josh FitzGerald, and Chris Gilbert with Victorian and Tasmanian roots, Archier creates elegantly minimal architecture, furniture, and lighting.

Jake Stollery
Illustrator

Jake Stollery's work intersects the lines between fashion, art, and technology. It draws inspiration from a mix of 90s cyberpunk, dusty science fiction, and new media experiments.

NGV International P.014

Federation Square P.018

Tim Sutherland
Creative director, StudioBrave

Tim Sutherland is the founder and creative director of StudioBrave, a creative agency devoted to unique and distinctive brand design.

Carlton Gardens P.020

Tim White
Director

Tim White is a commercial and music video director who spends half his time in Melbourne and the other half working abroad. His clients include Honda and the City of Tokyo.

Michael Drescher
Associate director, DKO

I am an architect and interior designer. I have been captivated by Melbourne's many unique layers since moving here years ago. As a lover of food and design, this city is perfect.

Melbourne Cricket Ground P.019

Manchester Unity Building P.022

Simone Speet & Emma Holder, *Büro North*

Büro North designer Simone is originally from Sydney whereas Emma is an ex-Wellingtonian. They both moved to Melbourne to experience its cultural, creative, and sporting atmosphere.

Abbotsford Convent
P.024

Alexandra Kovac
Fashion designer

I run a boutique womenswear label called Oracles. I also DJ in a duo called Rainbow Connection. We play fun boogie and disco music around town.

Juliet Burnett
Dancer

I am a ballet dancer, writer, and activist for the environment as well as human and animal rights. I was a senior artist at The Australian Ballet and will now continue my dancing career overseas.

Forum Melbourne
P.023

Fitzroy Backstreets
P.026

Hanna Richardson & Katherine Kemp, *ZWEI*

ZWEI is an architectural and interior practice that believes in the creation of authentic, sensorial, and experiential spaces with a strong narrative and sense of personality.

Moonee Ponds Creek Trail
P.028

Pandarosa
Creative studio

Pandarosa is made up of Ariel and Andii. Our main objective is to give the mundane wall, brochure or inanimate object life, blood, and a heart.

Phil Ferguson
Artist

I mainly create crocheted hats and post them on Instagram as @chiliphilly, an account I started to make new friends with after I moved to Melbourne from Perth.

Nicholas Building
P.027

Keith Haring Mural
P.029

1 ## NGV International

Map I, P.107

The custodian of a trove of important art from
Europe, Asia, America, and Oceania, NGV International's architecture by key Modernist figure
Sir Roy Grounds (1905–1981) is as mesmerising
as its blockbuster exhibitions. Although its
original exterior and recent interior remodel-
ling work by Mario Bellini are outstanding
in their own right, the star of the show is its
Leonard French–designed stained glass ceiling – one of the largest pieces of suspended
stained glass in the world. Head over on a Friday night for live performances, pop-up events,
and after-hours access to exhibitions.

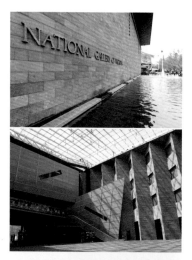

🕙 1000–1700 daily   🏠 180 St Kilda Rd., Southbank
📞 +61 (0)3 8620 2222   URL www.ngv.vic.gov.au
🖉 Free guided tours available. Exhibition
admission fees may apply. Book via website.

*"One of our favourite haunts is the gallery containing
the collection of Mesoamerican sculptures and
decorative arts."*

– Hannah & David Constantine, Studio Constantine

2 University of Melbourne
Map D, P.105

Founded in 1853, the University of Melbourne is Australia's second oldest university and boasts an aesthetically pleasing blend of period architecture and contemporary design. Amongst the latest additions is the Faculty of Architecture, Building, and Planning building jointly done by John Wardle Architects and NADAAA. The South Lawn underground car park which was built in 1972 is Australia's first fully enclosed subterranean landscape, featuring a forest of concrete columns that function as a stormwater drainage system. A scene from the original Mad Max film was also filmed here.

🏠 Grattan St., Parkville
📞 +61 (0)3 9035 5511
URL www.unimelb.edu.au

"Our favourite part of the university is the South Lawn underground car park, which looks like a cross between a vast Gothic crypt and a dystopian cityscape."

– Chris Haddad, Josh FitzGerald & Chris Gilbert, Archier

3 Federation Square

Fed Square, as the locals call it, is Melbourne's cultural epicentre. Occupying a prime location beside the Yarra River, Botanic Gardens, and Flinders Street station, the 3.8-hectare space features a unique system of spatial and surface geometries – designed by LAB Architecture and local firm Bates Smart – that allows for individual buildings to stand out on their own while uniting as a visual whole. Sandstone, glass, and zinc were the three materials used prominently in constuction to give the place its distinct look. Sign up for a public programme at the square or ACMI for a fulfilling day out.

🕑 💲 *Check online for programme info*
🏠 *Corner of Swanston & Flinders St., CBD*
📞 *+61 (0)3 9655 1900* URL *fedsquare.com*
📘 *@FedSquare* 🔗 *ACMI: www.acmi.net.au*

"*The architecture's complexity and details still blow my mind every time I see it. Also, it's right next to Hosier Lane with constantly evolving street art.*"

– Jake Stollery

④ Melbourne Cricket Ground
Map C, P.105

Built in 1853, less than 20 years after Melbourne was founded, the MCG is a spiritual place for Melburnian sports lovers and has been dubbed the 'beating heart' of the Aussie football-obsessed city. Home to the latter sport since 1859, it was also the birthplace of test cricket in 1877, one-day international cricket in 1971, as well as the main stadium for the 1956 Olympic Games and 2006 Commonwealth Games. Architecturally, its historical significance is aligned with its contemporary updates. On a non-event day, book a guided tour to learn more about Australia's sporting heritage at the inner sanctum and the National Sports Museum (NSM).

🕑 *Opening hours vary with events*
🏠 *Brunton Ave., Richmond*
📞 *+61 (0)3 9657 8888* URL *www.mcg.org.au*
📎 *75-min guided tours: 1000-1500 daily except certain PH. Book via website. NSM: nsm.org.au*

"*Go with a local to an AFL game so they can explain it, a blockbuster like the Anzac Day game between Collingwood and Essendon, or the Grand Final.*"

– Tim Sutherland, StudioBrave

5 Carlton Gardens & Royal Exhibition Building

Map A, P.102

Erected for the 1880 Melbourne International Exhibition, the World Heritage Site-listed Carlton Gardens and Royal Exhibition Building are ideally located between the CBD, Carlton, and Fitzroy. The northern section of the former holds the museum, tennis courts, and a children's playground designed as a Victorian maze, while the southern section harbours a picturesque fountain and duck ponds. The Royal Exhibition Building at the centre is a meld of Byzantine, Romanesque, Lombardic, and Italian-Renaissance styles designed by Joseph Reed; and looks especially impressive at night.

🕐 💲 *Royal Exhibition Building: Open for exhibitions only. Check website for info.* 🏠 *1-111 Carlton St., Carlton* 🔗 *www.melbourne.vic.gov.au/parks, museumsvictoria.com.au/reb*

"I personally prefer the southern half of the Gardens as it gets more sunlight in the later hours of the day."

– Tim White

6 Manchester Unity Building
Map B, P.104

Melbourne's iconic Manchester Unity Building may have been completed in 1932, but its Neo-Gothic architecture and visceral materiality never fail to catch the eye even after all these years. Besides its design, its construction process was also a remarkable human feat; featuring generous amounts of steel, marble, mother-of-pearl glazed terracotta (or faience) tiles, and towering plate-glass windows to reinvigorate a city that was shackled by economic depression. It is usually open to the public during the Melbourne open house event, so mark your calendars.

🏠 220 Collins St., CBD
☎ +61 (0)3 9663 5494
URL manchesterunitybuilding.com.au
🖉 Open House Melbourne:
www.openhousemelbourne.org

"The way the materials meet and interact with each other is inspiring. Keep an eye out for the six-metre original boardroom table that has survived all the building's refurbishments."

– Michael Drescher, DKO

7 Forum Melbourne

Map B, P.105

Formerly Melbourne's State Theatre, the Forum is one of the city's most renowned landmarks. It features striking Gothic and Middle Eastern influences that have cut an impressive figure into the skyline since 1929. Inside, its incredible sound system and interiors make for a wonderful venue to take in a wide array of live entertainment acts and concerts. Upon your visit, be sure to look at the faithful reproductions of Greco-Roman statuary and the twinkling ceiling that replicates twilight. Tickets typically sell out quickly, so book well in advance.

🕐 *Opening hours & admission fees vary with programmes*
📞 *1300 111 011* 🏠 *154 Flinders St., CBD*
🔗 *forummelbourne.com.au*
🎫 *Tickets: www.ticketmaster.com.au*

"With a pumping sound system and impressive architecture inside and out, the Forum is the best place to experience local and international theatre and music."

– Simone Speet & Emma Holder, Büro North

8 Abbotsford Convent

Map P, P.109

Since 1842, the Abbotsford Convent has evolved from a politician's home into a convent and, finally, the community hub that it is today. A short bicycle ride away from the CBD, it is a perfect union of countryside vibes and a convenient location, featuring an extensive programme of events throughout the year for every age. Drop by The Farm and Café for its delicious fresh produce or community-favourite restaurant Lentil As Anything for some mouthwatering vegetarian food. In the summertime, the place comes to life with night markets, parties, and outdoor performances.

🕐 0730–2200 daily
🏠 1 St Heliers St., Abbotsford
📞 +61 (0)3 9415 3600
URL abbotsfordconvent.com.au

"Make sure you take a walk along the Yarra trail to Dights Falls and back – it's magic!"

– Alexandra Kovac, Oracles

9 Fitzroy Backstreets
Map A, P.103

Created in 1839, the Fitzroy suburb has long
been associated with the working class and is
currently home to a wide variety of ethnicities
and socio-economic groups. Not surprisingly, it
is also the site of an ever-evolving outdoor gallery of street art. Take a walk around the backstreets between Brunswick, Smith, Gertrude,
and Johnston Streets and find yourself surrounded by spray-painted graffiti, murals, and
stencil art created by local and international
artists. The area also boasts an eclectic mix of
architecture ranging from bluestone miner's
cottages to iron-lace bedecked terraces and
rustic warehouses. Get your camera ready.

🏠 *Backstreets between Brunswick, Smith,*
Gertrude, and Johnston St., Fitzroy

"Let yourself get lost, and walk down every tiny
laneway and tree-lined street you come across to see
the best street art."

– Juliet Burnett

10 Nicholas Building
Map B, P.104

Designed by architect Harry Norris (1888–1966), the Nicholas Building continues to capture the creative hearts and minds of Melbourne. Originally built during the period in which the Flinders Lane garment trade was thriving, its space is now divided into studios used by artists, designers, and makers alike. Influenced by the Chicago and Greek-Revival style, the architecture features a grey terracotta faience façade, ionic pilasters, and towering columns. Browse around each floor for glimpses into the city's coolest workshops and studios.

🕐 *Opening hours vary by tenant*
🏠 *37 Swanston St., CBD*
URL *nicholasbuilding.org.au*
f *@nicholasbuildingassociation*

"*Enter through the old lift, wander the halls, and look into the various studios. If you go to an Open Studio event, you can purchase directly from the artist.*"
– Hanna Richardson & Katherine Kemp, ZWEI

11 Moonee Ponds Creek Trail
Map T, P.110

Running through urban Melbourne, with a part
of it stretching alongside and underneath the
CityLink, the Moonee Ponds Creek Trail provides
a unique view into the underbelly of the inner
city freeway. As you depart from Docklands
and head north towards Brunswick West, you
will come across concrete storm drains that
were once canals for coal barges before modern realignment work. Recent habitat conser-
vation efforts have also brought native flora
and fauna like Pobblebonk Frogs and Nankeen
Night Herons to the upper catchment area –
sights that are best enjoyed by foot or bike.

🏠 *Docklands Dr., Docklands to Hope St.,*
Brunswick West

"Always look up. It really helps in getting a sense of scale
and placement about the bizarreness of this location,
although doing this while riding might be tricky."

– Ariel & Andii, Pandarosa

12 Keith Haring Mural
Map A, P.103

Pop art legend Keith Haring (1958–1990) was an American artist whose grafitti-like work remains revered to this day. Influencing and iconic of New York City street culture in the 1980s, his instantly recognisable bold line drawings can be seen on only 31 known murals that still exist to this day all over the world – with the one in Collingwood being a fan favourite. Over the years, it has been restored to its original vibrancy and vitality, playing a part in retaining the suburb's character and charm.

🏠 *35 Johnston St., Collingwood*

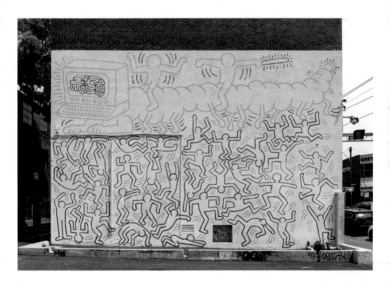

"I really love the Keith Haring mural because it is really amazing to have a large artwork by an incredibly famous queer artist so publicly available for all to see."

– Phil Ferguson

Cultural & Art Spaces

Housemuseums, revered cinemas, and carbon-neutral craft

Melbourne's culture and arts scene is a diverse, vibrant, and fla-vourful mix of festivals, exhibitions, and live performances that cover everything from musicals, plays, theatre, concerts, ballet, and comedy shows to contemporary, classical, and indigenous arts, crafts, and sculptures – hosted by a wide variety of creative-friendly spaces peppered all over the city. Venues range from those with leafy outdoor settings like Heide (#13) and The Abbotsford Convent (#8) to more urbanised and modern places such as the Rooftop Bar and Cinema (#22). The city also seems to have at least one festival happening every other day, such as the world-famous Melbourne International Comedy Festival (*www.comedyfestival.com.au*), the Melbourne International Film Festival (*miff.com.au*), and Midsumma Festival (*midsumma.org.au*), amongst its countless food, wine, and cultural happenings. Many of the suburbs have their own street party scene also – the biggest being the St Kilda Festival, typically in February, which gathers more than 250,000 people by the beach for some good vibes. Should you decide to take a drive down the picturesque Great Ocean Road after exploring the neighbourhoods, make a pit stop at Qdos (*www.qdosarts.com*). Its Lorne site features a spectacular sculpture gallery in the forest for you to explore.

Lyon Housemuseum, P.036

Paris Thomson
Founder, SIRAP

Born and bred in Melbourne and travelling the world often with camera in hand, Paris is a film director with a love for wine, cheese, and considered design.

Lyon House-museum P.036

Laura Phillips
Editor, Open Journal

A Melbourne native, Laura Phillips founded Mr. Wolf Magazine, a journal of Nordic design, and is now the editor of Open Journal, a publication on architecture, urbanism, and design.

Virginia Martin
Fashion designer

I am the owner and designer of the womenswear label, búl. I focus on minimalistic yet classic shapes, easy-to-wear relaxing fits, and luxe fabrics.

Heide Museum of Modern Art P.034

Robin Boyd Foundation P.037

Ben Grosz & Laura Camilleri, *Grosz Co.Lab*

When not running their design consultancy, the pair travel the world on design-led excursions to continue inspiring their diverse creative practice.

Daine Singer P.040

Alice Oehr
Designer & illustrator

I am a designer and illustrator living in Melbourne with my sister and my cat. I love to go out and soak up the atmosphere of Melbourne – there is always something on.

Antonia Sellbach
Artist & musician

Antonia Sellbach is known for her large-scale abstract paintings. She is also a musician with local bands Love of Diagrams and Beaches; and co-founded feminist project, LISTEN.

ACCA P.038

Craft Victoria P.041

Beci Orpin
Designer, illustrator & author

I have released three DIY books and in 2015, my first children's book. I live in Melbourne with my husband Raph, sons Tyke and Ari, and two British shorthair cats Tio and Miso.

BUS Projects
P.043

Mikala Tai
Curator, Supergraph

I mainly work in contemporary art, fashion, and also run Supergraph, Melbourne's contemporary graphic art fair. I believe good design makes every day a little more special.

Abigail Crompton
Director, Third Drawer Down

I am a director of a product design studio, a wholesaler, and a retailer. I collaborate with artists and museums worldwide; focusing on the challenges posed by cultural retailing.

Lamington Drive
P.042

Bird's Basement
P.044

Bliss & Bonnie Adams
Founders, Marble Basics

We are sisters born and bred in Melbourne. We design marble homeware for our label Marble Basics. Our designs are functional, timeless, and we pride them on simplicity.

The Astor Theatre
P.046

Lola Berry
Nutritionist

I am a nutritionist, author, and yogi nerd. I work in media writing and also talk on radio and TV about health and loving every second of it. I am all about living the best life you can.

Tooth and Claw
Video production house

Tooth and Claw is a boutique video production company specialising in musically driven video works. We love what we do and play well with others.

Rooftop Cinema
P.045

St Kilda Twilight Market
P.047

13 Heide Museum of Modern Art
Map V, P.110

A 20-minute drive from the CBD will take you to the Heide Museum of Modern Art, where John and Sunday Reed used to live and receive artists, writers, and intellectuals. The couple were noted for their relentless support of Australian art, and as their collection outgrew their first residence (Heide I), they commissioned a second home (Heide II) in 1964 as a "gallery to be lived in". Since it opened its doors to the public in 1981, the Heide remains a temple for modern and contemporary art, and a popular destination to escape the city grind. Allow a good two to three hours to take everything in.

🕐 1000–1700 (Tu–Su) [Café Heide: 0900–] 💲 $20/Free for 16–
🏠 7 Templestowe Rd., Bulleen
📞 +61 (0)3 9850 1500
🌐 www.heide.com.au
🎫 Free guided tours: 1400 (Tu–Su)

"*Round your trip off by settling into a long lunch at the café. Grab an Uber for the drive there and back if you're planning to settle into a few drinks!*"
– Paris Thomson, SIRAP

14 Lyon Housemuseum
Map W, P.110

As you cross the threshold of the Original Housemuseum, you will also be entering Corbett and Yueji Lyon's home. Citing influences from a lineage of private collections in domestic settings, such as the Frick Collection in New York and the Peggy Guggenheim Collection in Venice, collector and architect Corbett designed the double-height complex to showcase paintings, sculptures, and installations by the likes of Howard Arkley and Patricia Piccinini. Although it is currently only accessible via pre-booked visits, the Galleries next door are open to the public from Tuesday to Sunday (10am to 5pm).

🕐 By appointment only   💲 $25
🏠 219 Cotham Rd., Kew   📞 +61 (0)3 9817 2300
URL www.lyonhousemuseum.com.au
🖉 Check website for booking info.

"The juxtaposition of walking through their well-designed kitchen and looking at superb art, brings home that art is something to be lived in and surrounded by in daily life."

– Virginia Martin, búl

15 Robin Boyd Foundation

Map G, P.107

In continuing the architect's compelling ethos and long-running dedication to progressing the international Modern Movement in the Australian architectural scene, the Robin Boyd Foundation organises expansive learning programmes to provide rare insights into the country's mid-century cultural shift. These programmes include open days, forums, and performances that take place at the Walsh Street home that Boyd 'built' for his family and brought him into prominence in 1958. Take in the benefits of good spatial design as you enter the house.

🏠 290 Walsh St., South Yarra
📞 +61 (0)3 9820 9838 **URL** robinboyd.org.au
📘 @robinboydfoundation 🔗 Guided tour: $35.
Check online for tour & programme info.

"Tours can be arranged with afternoon tea."
– Laura Phillips, Open Journal

16 ACCA
Map I, P.107

Clad in a singular rusty steel façade, the ACCA building was developed by local architects Wood Marsh in 2002 as 'a sculpture in which to show art'. Based on the European model of the Kunsthalle, ACCA is now one of Melbourne's leading contemporary art spaces, bringing the latest and most significant artwork by artists from around the world to Melbourne audiences for free. Look out for 'Vault' – a steel plate sculpture by Ron Robertson-Swann on the ACCA grounds which was dubbed the 'Yellow Peril' for the uproar its original placement caused within the community.

🕑 1000–1700 (Tu–F), 1100– (Sa–Su)
🏠 111 Sturt St., Southbank
📞 +61 (0)3 9697 9999
f @acca.melbourne
URL acca.melbourne

"The building and the ever-changing work that it houses are well worth a visit."

– Ben Grosz & Laura Camilleri, Grosz Co.Lab

17 Daine Singer
Map A, P.102

Previously a gallery manager at the reputable
Anna Schwartz Gallery and curator at the
National Gallery of Victoria, independent curator
Daine Singer has widely been recognised as
one of the hottest talents in the city's artsphere.
Currently, her gallery represents a circle of ex-
citing Australian contemporary artists, including
Minna Gilligan, Zoë Croggon, and Andrew
McQualter. Past exhibitions have projected a
careful balance between boundary-pushing
experimental art and more commercial work
across multiple mediums.

🕐 *1200–1700 (W–F), –1600 (Sa)*
🏠 *Rear 90 Moor St., Fitzroy*
📞 *+61 (0)410 264 036*
🔗 *www.dainesinger.com*
📘 *@dainesinger*

*"It is one of Melbourne's best galleries, filled with
cutting-edge work by both emerging and
established artists."*

– Antonia Sellbach

18 Craft Victoria
Map B, P.105

Craft Victoria's galleries are a design lover's dream-come-true. A non-profit organisation backed by a friendly team of staff who are all artists themselves, it represents local talented contemporary ceramicists, jewellery makers, glassblowers, weavers, and woodworkers regularly demonstrating new ideas and techniques that revive traditional crafts. Besides rotating exhibitions, the venue also houses a retail space full of inspiring work where you can pick up beautiful sourvenirs.

🕐 1100-1800 (M-F), -1600 (Sa)
🏠 Watsons Plc., Off Flinders Ln., CBD
📞 +61 (0)3 9650 7775
🌐 www.craft.org.au
📷 @craftvictoria

"Wander into this great place to buy something that is really beautiful, totally unique, and locally made."

–Alice Oehr

19 Lamington Drive

Map A, P.103

Pop by independent agency The Jacky Winter
Group's headquarters and its exhibition room
all in one go. Since 2008, Lamington Drive has
established itself as a gallery space that represents and showcases the artwork of commercial cartoonists, photographers, artists, and
designers from all walks of life. Try to align your
visit with an opening night, which usually falls
on a Wednesday and always includes yummy
lamingtons (a traditional Australian dessert),
refreshing beverages, and good conversations.

🕐 1100-1800 (W-F), 1200-1700 (Sa)
🏠 52 Budd St., Collingwood
📞 +61 (0)3 8060 9745
URL lamingtondrive.com
📷 @lamingtondrive

*"Check when they have openings – they are usually
a fun night when they are on. Also, the artwork here
is often edition-based and quite affordable."*
– Beci Orpin

20 BUS Projects
Map A, P.103

With a revolving roster of excellent shows, this artist-run initiative has a finger on the pulse of the city's artistic beat. Beginning in 2001 as a design collective and project space, BUS now promotes and collaborates with Australian artists across a wide range of mediums. Located at a former mid-20th century paint factory, which was re-designed by John Wardle Architects who work next door, BUS also operates outside of traditional gallery contexts, developing exhibitions, events, and performances off-site. Check online for programme updates.

🕐 1200–1800 (Tu–F), 1000–1600 (Sa)
🏠 25-31 Rokeby St., Collingwood
📞 +61 (0)3 9995 8359
URL www.busprojects.org.au
f @busprojects

"The café (Lemon Middle & Orange) next door provides you with a great coffee hit!"

– Mikala Tai, Supergraph

21 Bird's Basement
Map B, P.104

Although it was only set up in 2016, Bird's Basement has been deemed the best jazz club in Melbourne by true fans. A reincarnation of New York City's legendary live venue Birdland, the purpose-built space with flawless acoustics and 'no bad seats' provides the perfect stage for local and international acts in the genre to shine. Besides hosting five weekly gigs, it also offers an intimate ambience for dining and drinks within its cosy and cavernous interior. Reservations or programme ticket purchases are highly recommended before you go.

🕐 1800 till late (W–Su). Check online for programme info. 🏠 11 Singers Lane, CBD 📞 +61 1300 225 299
🔗 birdsbasement.com 📘📷 @birdsbasement

"Usually, there are two seatings for popular musicians. I would recommend the second session so you can hang out afterwards."

– Abigail Crompton, Third Drawer Down

22 Rooftop Cinema @Curtin House

Map B, P.104

The open-air Rooftop Cinema is a much-loved Melburnian institution atop Curtin House, right in the heart of the CBD. As its name suggests, the cinema is nestled seven storeys above the ground and fitted out with deck chairs as well as a projector that screens a diverse selection of films, ranging from obscure art house and classic 80s to recent thrillers and dramas. The adjoining Rooftop Bar is usually open to serve you a cheeky drink or two before your show. Even in the summer, it can get pretty chilly so be sure to have some warm clothes on hand.

🕐 *Check online for programme info*
💲 *$22+ booking fee incl. GST*
🏠 *Curtin House, 252 Swanston St., CBD*
🔗 *www.rooftopcinema.com.au*
📘 *@rooftopcinemamelbourne*
🔗 *Rooftop Bar: rooftopbar.co*

"*It's the best way to soak in Melbourne's skyline. Go at sunset and get there early to get the best seats. Head downstairs to Cookie after for delicious modern Thai.*"

– Bliss & Bonnie Adams, Marble Basics

 **The Astor Theatre**

Map R, P.109

Renowned for its repertory programme and collection of classic, modern, and cult movies, The Astor Theatre is a grand historic art-deco cinema with stalls and a dress circle that opened its doors in 1936. It is the last single-screen cinema of its kind still operating in Melbourne and one of only a few left in the world. The only part of the Astor that is not old-fashioned is its state-of-the-art audio-visual system. Pick any movie from their calendar and prepare for an enthralling experience.

🕐 **S** *Check online for programme info*
🏠 *Corner of Chapel St. & Dandenong Rd., St Kilda*
📞 *+61 (0)3 9510 1414*
URL *www.astortheatre.net.au*
f *@astortheatre* 🔗 *Book via website.*

"The cream of Melbourne cinemas – it has been saved from closure many times by local cine-philes. Check out the website well in advance."

– Tooth and Claw

24 St Kilda Twilight Market

Map N, P.109

During the summer, the St Kilda Twilight Market brings the community together on Thursday evenings to a beautiful beachside location beneath the palm trees with live music in the air. Brimming with stalls selling a wonderful array of artwork, vintage wear, crafts, handmade clothes and accessories, as well as food and drink from all corners of the world, it is the place to be for authentic slices of local life. Go there with an empty stomach and eat on the go as you browse around for souvenirs.

🕐 1700–2200 (Th) [Dec–Feb]
🏠 O'Donnell Gardens, St Kilda
📞 +61 (0)403 119 998
URL stkildatwilightmarket.com
f @stkildatwilightmarket

"This is super rustic and has such a great vibe. Added bonus: brilliant food. Get there in time to watch the sunset – it's pretty special."

– Lola Berry

Incu

Acne Studios
adidas
A.P.C.
Ashby
COMMON PROJECTS
CONVERSE
Cote&Ciel
KLOKE
LARSSON & JENNINGS
Libertine-Libertine
MAISON KITSUNE
NIKE
SPORTSWEAR
NORSE PROJECTS
Oliver Spencer
OUR LEGACY
Paul Smith
JEANS
rag & bone
RAINS
RICHER POORER
SATURDAYS
SURF NYC
ALEXANDER WANG
the
Hill-side
VANISHING
ELEPHANT
Weathered

Markets & Shops

Homegrown labels, curated lifestyle products, andweekend markets

Shopping enthusiasts will be spoilt for choice by the variety of boutiques, stores, and markets spread out across Melbourne. From the culinary delights and fresh produce found at the Queen Victoria Market (*qvm.com.au*) in the CBD and the 'one man's trash is another man's treasure' ethos of the Camberwell Sunday Market (#35) to the earth-friendly, sustainability-focused St Andrews Market (#36) in the bushy outskirts, every location offers a unique and memorable experience. If you love to buck the trend, be sure to check out local labels like Lucy Folk (#32) or Incu (#26), while Third Drawer Down (#25) offers unique art and design products that will make stylish additions to your life. Bargain hunters can enjoy designerwear at knock-down prices at DFO (*www.dfo.com.au/south-wharf*), whereas hipsters can head over to the vintage clothing stores in Brunswick and Fitzroy to find true gems. Other shopping strips that are brimming with stores include the stretch of Chapel Street, which starts with more commercial brands around Toorak Road and grows more eclectic towards Dandenong Road where there are lots of independent designer and streetwear stores. Coburg is also a cultural wonderland with one-of-their-kind shops offering everything from elaborate wedding dresses and jewellery to more eccentric and exotic goods. Spend a productive day there by shopping, people-watching, and fuelling up along the way with exquisite Middle Eastern cuisine along Sydney Road.

Ellen Porteus
Graphic designer & illustrator

I am obsessed with crazy co-lourful palettes, surreal patterns, and clever illustrations with a sense of humour!

Incu
P.054

Motherbird
Creative studio

Motherbird was founded by Jack Mussett, Dan Evans, and Chris Murphy in 2009. The creative studio has worked with MTV, Qantas, Nickelodeon, and Mush-room Music.

Julian Frost
Animator & illustrator

I am from New Zealand and now live in Melbourne. My job involves drawing and animating silly things.

Third
Drawer
Down
P.052

Dixons
Recycled
Records
P.055

Ellie Malin
Printmaker

Inspired by a love for travel and beautiful moments in life, my artworks reflect a playful approach to image-making where bright colours and forms construct the landscape.

Mr Kitly
P.058

Allison Colpoys & Kasia Gadecki, *The Souvenir Society*

Allison Colpoys and Kasia Gadecki met at university back in the Y2K and instantly bonded over their love for pattern, illus-tration, packaging, and design.

Penny Min Ferguson
Designer & illustrator

Penny Min Ferguson is the human behind Min Pin, an illustration-based design label specialising in jewellery, ceram-ics, and textiles.

Modern
Times
P.056

Guild of
Objects
P.059

Michaela Webb
Creative director, Studio Round

Michaela co-founded design studio Round. She is responsible for creatively leading the studio's diverse projects.

Lucy Folk
P.061

Paul Troon
Graphic designer

Having worked at Mahon & Band, Design By Pidgeon, and Australian skincare brand Aesop, I now run design studio Ultra with my friend Kate Rogers.

Mildred & Duck
Graphic design studio

Creative directors Daniel Smith and Sigiriya Brown design for print, digital, and environmental media; creating solutions for a variety of sectors that communicate and connect with people.

Gertrude
Street
P.060

Dinosaur
Designs
P.062

Brett Phillips
Founder & CEO, 3 Deep

By identifying the need for strategic and entrepreneurial thinkers beyond the provision of creative services, Brett has established 3 Deep as a prominent innovative business.

Camberwell
Sunday
Market
P.064

Alexandra de Boer
Graphic designer, Elenberg Fraser

Alexandra is a graphic designer specialising in publication design, typography, branding, and wayfinding.

Wona Bae & Charlie Lawler, *Founders, Loose Leaf*

Loose Leaf is a botanical design studio and retail space of indoor plants and fresh cut flowers, set in a beautifully converted warehouse in Melbourne.

Wunder-
kammer
P.063

St Andrews
Market
P.065

25 Third Drawer Down
Map A, P.103

Third Drawer Down is not your typical gift store – it stocks a wide range of fun and hard-to-find artist-made objects, homeware, books, jewellery, and eccentric odds-and-ends, sourced locally and internationally by its dedicated team. Its stores are independent concept destinations that curate goods based on the brand's interpretation of the traditional museum or gallery store. It also stocks items produced by the in-house design studio, which creates artist-licensed items and bespoke ranges for cultural institutions.

🕑 Fitzroy: 1000–1700 (M, Sa), –1800 (Tu–F), 1100–1600 (Su)
🏠 93 George St., Fitzroy
📞 + 61 (0)3 9534 4088
URL www.thirddrawerdown.com
f ⓘ @thirddrawerdown

"If you see something you like but can't take it home with you, their online store ships internationally."
– Ellen Porteus

26 Incu

The innovative brainchild of brothers Brian and Vincent Wu, Incu was born out of their love of travel and international brands, as well as a desire to showcase upcoming Aussie talent. The fashion and lifestyle product retailer first opened their doors in 2002 and now own several branches across Melbourne, Sydney, and Queensland. Its Albert Coates Lane location caters mostly to men, but its Chadstone Shopping Centre location carries more varied stock.

🕐 *Opening hours & contact info vary by location*
URL *www.incu.com*
f *@incuclothing*
📷 *@incu_clothing*

"Incu is opposite our studio, so we often find ourselves going out for a coffee and returning with a wardrobe of clothes."

– Jack Mussett, Dan Evans & Chris Murphy, Motherbird

27 Dixons Recycled Records
Map H, P.107

Dixons Recycled Records is one of the longest
running second-hand music stores in Australia
- renowned as a great source of bargain goods
and hard-to-find items. It buys and sells used
LP records, CDs, vintage Hi-Fis, magazines,
as well as other obscure collectibles, next to
an extensive library of indie, punk, rock, pop,
dance, metal, country, blues, and experimental
sounds. Look out for the following local recom-
mendations: The Ninnies (bush folk), Mountain
Maggot (punk), Born Hungry (ska-metal), Dar-
ren and the Pubes (pub rock).

🕓 Fitzroy: 0930-1800 (M-Th), -1900 (F), 1000-1800
(Sa), 1100- 1700 (Su) 🏠 414 Brunswick St., Fitzroy
📞 +61 (0)3 9416 2272 URL www.dixons.com.au
📘 @dixonsrecycledrecords

*"My favourite souvenir when travelling is CDs.
Find an album from a popular local band for an
insight into local culture."*

– Julian Frost

28 Modern Times
Map A, P.103

Modern Times is a mecca of mid-century modern designs. It started out as a series of pop-up shops in 2010 but has now become a permanent fixture in the city's vintage furniture scene, boasting choice vintage Danish furniture alongside locally made homeware and art specially picked to complement the style. The sprawling store space houses everything from highly collectable Danish pieces in teak and rosewood by celebrated designers such as Hans Wegner and Arne Vodder, to small gifts lovingly handcrafted by local talents.

🕐 1000-1800 (M-F), -1700 (Sa), 1100- (Su)
🏠 311 Smith St., Fitzroy   📞 +61 (0)3 9913 8598
URL www.moderntimes.com.au
📘 @ModTimes   📷 @moderntimesau

"Stop next door at Shop Ramen for a heart-warming noodle soup or cross the road to Alimentari for a delicious meal."

– Ellie Malin

29 Mr Kitly
Map K, P.108

Named after its owner Bree Claffey's cat, Mr Kitly is akin to a secret garden tucked away in a Victorian-era building. The light- and greenery-filled store, gallery, and architecture studio is particularly noted for the thoughtful and considered collection of functional objects in ceramic, wood, metal, textiles, and fibres on display – all with a strong nod to Japanese aesthetics. It also stocks a wide range of books related to crafts, design, and architecture. If there is an ongoing exhibition, the local or international artist's works are often available for purchase as well.

🕐 1100–1800 (M, W–F), –1600 (Su), 1000–1700 (Sa)
🏠 1/F, 381 Sydney Rd., Brunswick
📞 +61 (0)3 9078 7357 URL mrkitly.com.au
📘 @MrKitly 📷 @mrkitly

"We love this store – it will serve all of your present-buying needs."

– Allison Colpoys & Kasia Gadecki, The Souvenir Society

30 Guild of Objects
Map A, P.103

Affectionately known as the Guild, this cute little store in North Melbourne is run by three small-batch potters. Brooke Thorn, Chela Edmunds, and Tao Oudomvilay set it up in 2015 as a way for them to not only share their own projects, but also showcase the work of other talented artists and makers within the local community. Besides housing an amazing array of unique and beautiful ceramics, jewellery, and textiles that are proudly made in Australia, Guild also hosts crafting workshops by local craftspeople. Check online to book a spot.

🕐 1100-1600 (W-Sa) 🏠 35 Smith St., Fitzroy
📞 +61 (0)401 035 157 🔗 guildofobjects.com
📘 @Guildofobjects 📷 @guildofobjects

"This is a great place to pick up a souvenir and support local designers."

– Penny Min Ferguson, Min Pin

31 Gertrude Street
Map A, P.103

Gertrude Street is one of Melbourne's many shopping strips that can be found a short stroll or tram ride away from the city. The diverse area is filled with boutiques and F&B options that brim with character and charm. Fuel up with coffee and arepas at Sonido before making your way to Bruce, Obus, Handsom, The Standard Store, and Third Drawer Down (#25). Marvel at the weird and wonderful treasure trove of costumes that is Rose Chong, then complete your trip with dinner at Cutler & Co., cocktails at The Everleigh, or sake at Tamura's .

🏠 Gertrude St., Fitzroy
URL sonido.com.au, shopbruce.com.au, obus.com.au, www.handsom-store.com, www.rosechong.com, www.cutlerandco.com.au, theeverleigh.com, tamurasakebar.com

"Make a booking at Cutler & Co.!"
– Michaela Webb, Studio Round

32 Lucy Folk
Map B, P.105

From popcorn rings to corn chips on chains, Lucy Folk's original food-inspired jewellery range continues to gain her renown locally and beyond. In reflecting her passions for all things yummy and stylish, architect Charlie Inglis transformed her first store space on Crossley Street into a whimsical wonderland that frame her characterful collections perfectly. Although the eponymous brand has since grown into a global fashion and accessories destination with several other locations, the original outlet still retains its quirky charm, which you can now take in slowly with your coffee order.

🕐 1000–1700 (M–Sa), 1100– (Su) 🏠 1A Crossley St., CBD 📞 +61 (0)3 9663 6829 🔗 lucyfolk.com
📘 @lucyfolkjewellery 📷 @lucy_folk

"*Lucy Folk is a great place to get accessories good enough to eat. While you're there make sure you try some of the bars and cafés on Crossley Street.*"

– Daniel Smith & Sigiriya Brown, Mildred & Duck

33 Dinosaur Designs
Map B, P.104

Dinosaur Designs is an eclectic store packed with jewellery, homeware, and lifestyle products by Australian designers and life partners Louise Olsen and Stephen Ormandy. Since 1986, the talented duo has drawn inspiration from nature to use resin in creating stunning wearable pieces and objects that will spruce up any living space. All items are lovingly and sustainably made by hand in the Sydney studio by skilled artisans under the duo's direction.

🕐 1000–1800 (M–Th, Sa), –2000 (F), 1100–1700 (Su)
🏠 Shop T06, The Strand Melb., 250 Elizabeth St., CBD 📞 +61 (0)3 9650 8000
🔲 www.dinosaurdesigns.com.au
f @DinosaurDesigns 📷 @dinosaur_designs

"When travelling overseas and in need of a gift to take, I always gather a few of their one-off pieces as a slice of home to share with friends around the world."

– Paul Troon, Ultra

34 Wunderkammer
Map B, P.104

As one of Melbourne's shopping highlights, Wunderkammer is well-known for stocking rare and unusual items on their shelves, such as antique scientific instruments, vintage medical equipment, framed insects, taxidermied creatures, skeletons, and fossils. Its name is derived from the German expression for a 'cabinet of curiosities', which was also an old concept where people collected and displayed all kinds of oddities and one-of-a-kind items in wooden cabinets. A must-go for fans of curios.

🕙 1000-1800 (M-F), -1600 (Sa-Su)
🏠 439 Lonsdale St., CBD
📞 +61 (0)3 9642 4694
URL wunderkammer.com.au
f 🅾 @wunderkammermelbourne

"Take your time to browse the rare and the unusual."
— Brett Phillips, 3 Deep

35 Camberwell Sunday Market
Map X, P.110

The Camberwell Sunday Market sells only second-hand goods or hand-crafted items specifically made by the stall owner – excluding food. It is a great place to find vintage clothing, crockery, and books as well as unusual objects like vintage typewriters and ornaments, so you could easily spend a whole Sunday morning hunting for treasure and haggling to save a few dollars. Proceeds raised from the market will benefit a number of charities, so you would also be shopping for a good cause .

🕐 *0630–1230 (Su)*
🏠 *Marketplace, Camberwell*
🔗 *camberwellsundaymarket.org*
📘 *@CamberwellSundayMarket*
📷 *@camberwell_sunday_market*

"Make sure you get there early to experience the charm of the Camberwell Market, where treasures are endless and bargains are made to be haggled!"

– Alexandra de Boer, Elenberg Fraser

36 St Andrews Market
Map U, P.110

St Andrews Market is a vibrant Saturday market on the outskirts of Melbourne that has been a big part of the local community for over 40 years. With a focus on sustainability and the natural, it is a great place to relax and take in its bush setting while browsing for fresh, organic, handmade, recycled, or creative goods. Besides healthy and delicious food, there are also massage stations, hair braiding services, pony rides for kids, tai chi sessions, and live music for you to enjoy.

🕐 0900-1400 (Sa) except Total Fire Ban days
🏠 Kangaroo Ground-St Andrews Rd., St Andrews
📞 +61 (0)467 535 341
🔗 standrewsmarket.com.au
📘 @StAndrewsMarket
📷 @standrewsmarket

"There's nothing better than sipping a chai tea on the hill overlooking the market."

– Wona Bae & Charlie Lawler, Loose Leaf

Restaurants & Cafés

Multicultural culinary options, coffee houses, and modern cooking

Melbourne is not just known for being the food and coffee capital of Australia. It is also a global culinary hotspot, offering mouthwatering old and new cuisines that have been influenced by its rich multicultural and multi-ethnic history. Its original flavours were built upon those of its traditional indigenous owners – gradually added onto by the British settlers and ethnic groups that emigrated to the city following World War II from the Netherlands, Italy, and Greece. Following subsequent major conflicts, many Yugoslavian, Turkish, Lebanese, Vietnamese, and Cambodian people also migrated over, on top of the growing Chinese, Indian, and Sri Lankan communities. Each of them brought along the cooking styles of their homelands, resulting in the deliciously diverse mix of restaurants and cafés lining the streets of Melbourne that have inextricably woven themselves into its fabric of society today. Ethopian restaurants such as Abesha (*www.abesharestaurant.com.au*) have been steadily gaining renown over the years, whereas the Italian restaurants along Lygon Street in Carlton, Chinese eateries in Box Hill, and Vietnamese options around Abbotsford remain long-time local favourites. Melburnians also love catching up with loved ones over brunch at places like SOJO (#40), Monk Bodhi Dharma (#45), and Auction Rooms (#46). Naturally, coffee flows in most veins – a phenomenon that can be attributed to the city's colourful past as well. The brewing culture can be experienced in almost every suburb, where award-winning baristas are so dedicated to the art that they regularly retain Melbourne as one of the world's best coffee destinations every year.

Bardo
Design collaborative

Bardo is the collaborative experience of Bren Imboden and Luis Viale. They work with agencies, institutions, cultural events, start-ups, and established companies worldwide.

Parco Canteen P.071

Surya Prasetya
Founder & director, Studio SP-GD

At Studio SP-GD, we develop ideas and offer creative direction, branding, and identity solutions for various industries. In my spare time, I enjoy designing and making furniture and objects.

The Independent P.070

Sasha Heath
Hellotomato

Sasha is a Melbourne-based illustrator who started her own freelance studio called Hellotomato. She specialises in large-scale murals, illustrations, and ceramic cuteness.

SUPER-RANDOM P.072

Christopher Boots
Industrial designer

I run a humble studio focusing on creating beautiful and timeless lighting sculptures. I am inspired and driven by nature – crystals and quantum concepts are always on my mind.

Grub Fitzroy P.074

Charlie Romeo Brophy
Photographer

I am really just a tomboyish girl born in a concrete jungle, fulfilling a creative vision through photography and exploring mother nature in other parts of the world.

Livia Arena
Creative director, Livia Arena

I am the creative director of Livia Arena, my eponymous Australian women's fashion label. Established in 2011, its designs focus on relaxed styling with luxury finishes.

South of Johnston P.073

Carolina Café & Bar P.076

Billie Justice Thomson
Painter & illustrator

I specialise in reverse glass painting and have painted the windows of many shops in and around Melbourne. I particularly love food and nostalgic food imagery in my projects.

Estelle
P.078

Dom Bartolo & Ryan Guppy, *Founders, 21–19*

21–19 is a communications agency in Collingwood, Melbourne. We have been building stories that reach audiences, touch hearts, and influence minds since 2005.

Glenn Thomas
Illustrator

Glenn Thomas is an illustrator working under the alias The Fox And King. He is currently working on several commercial and personal projects.

Half Moon Café
P.077

Monk Bodhi Dharma
P.079

Jack Vanzet
Creative director & musician

I am a creative director and musician from Melbourne.

Cumulus Up
P.082

Alex & Tim Britten-Finschi, *FROM BRITTEN P/L*

The founders of the international menswear brand FROM BRITTEN have lived in Melbourne all their lives. They travel for work and the best food in every country they visit.

Fabio Ongarato
Founder, Fabio Ongarato Design

Fabio Ongarato Design is a multidisciplinary design studio. Their work is built on creative collaboration, strategic thinking, and a holistic approach to design.

Auction Rooms
P.080

Supernormal
P.083

 37 ## The Independent
Map Y, P.110

The Independent is ideally situated along the Dandenong Ranges in Melbourne's outskirts. With its high ceilings, spacious dining area, and exposed timber-and-brickwork, the restaurant retains the rustic charm of its building's former occupant – a vintage hardware store. Inspired by the seasons, fresh ingredients of the day, and chef Mauro Callegari's Argentinian roots, dishes here are designed for the whole table to share and enjoy. Outside, its herb-filled beer garden and kids' playing area make it the perfect destination for balmy summer evenings.

🕐 1730 till late (Th), 1200 till late (F–Su)
📍 79 Main St., Gembrook 📞 +61 (0)3 5968 1110
🔗 www.theindependentgembrook.com.au
📘📷 @TheIndependentGembrook
🔗 Reservations recommended. Book via website.

"*Don't miss the Provoleta. It's one of our favourite dishes – baked cheese with chimichurri.*"

– Bren Imboden & Luis Viale, Bardo

38 Parco Canteen
Map A, P.102

A tiny former power sub-station located on a traffic island in Carlton, Parco Canteen is a charming al fresco eatery offering scrumptious breakfast and lunch options amid a simple but stylish setting. Local favourites from the menu include the bánh mì with maple-glazed bacon, fried egg, and pickled carrot in a brioche bun, and the house-made granola with yoghurt, fresh apple, and rhubarb for the health-conscious. If you are lucky, you could be joined by some delightful furry company as you enjoy your meal at this dog-friendly café.

🕐 0730–1600 (M-F), 0830– (Sa-Su)
🏠 2 Argyle Place South, Carlton
📞 +61 (0)3 9348 1115 🌐 parco.com.au
📷 @parcocarlton

"They do the most delicious coffee and the best breakfast banh mi I've ever tasted! Sit in the sun and watch the world go by."

– Sasha Heath, Hellotomato

39 SUPERRANDOM
Map O, P.109

SUPERRANDOM is a cosy little café in Brighton that is much-loved by the neighbourhood for its full-bodied coffee and the delightful coffee art by its award-winning barista, Nobumasa Shimoyama. It only serves one blend – simply called 'coffee' – and fuss-free food that one can have on-the-go such as pastries, muffins, and sweet treats. If you are not in a hurry, dine in amid its simple yet thoughtful furnishings or enjoy your meal outdoors and people-watch The pressed jaffle sandwich comes highly recommended.

🕒 0630–1530 (Su–F), 0730– (Sa)
🏠 416 New St., Brighton
📞 +61 (0)3 9596 5987
f Super Random +Nobu

"Make sure you order a jaffle with your coffee."
– Surya Prasetya, Studio SP–GD

40. South of Johnston

Map A, P.103

South of Johnston or SOJO, as it is known, is an old valve-repackaging factory that has been completely transformed into a delightful dining destination by merging contemporary touches and sustainability with charming countryside vibes. The fruit trees and herbs outside the venue were planted with the intention of creating an urban orchard that the local community could benefit from. Inside, vintage knick-knacks, and an European fireplace add to its warm and welcoming ambience. SOJO's seasonal lunch menu caters for a variety of tastes and dietary requirements, featuring fresh ingredients daily.

🕐 0730-1700 (M-Su) 🏠 46 Oxford St., Collingwood 📞 +61 (0)3 9417 2741
URL www.southofjohnston.com.au
📘 📷 @SouthOfJohnston

"An excellent example of Melbourne's gastronomical options. Come early (before 10am) on the weekends if you don't want to wait too long!"

– Christopher Boots

41 Grub Fitzroy
Map A, P.102

Grub Fitzroy is an easy-going eatery set around a 1965 Airstream van. Its plant-filled al fresco dining area makes it the perfect spot to enjoy a meal or coffee on a clear and sunny day. During colder ones, you can stay warm and dry in the greenhouse, where fresh produce is grown as ingredients for the dishes served. Besides its delicious grub, patrons can delight in a great selection of beers and cocktails. If you are a music fan, keep an ear out for its fun playlist or check online to see if your visit could coincide with the live gig that occasionally takes place.

🕐 0800–1800 daily 🏠 87-89 Moor St., Fitzroy
📞 +61 (0)3 9419 8991 URL grubfitzroy.com.au
f 📷 @grubfitzroy

"Have a listen to their amazing radio documentary soundtrack."

– Livia Arena

42 Carolina Café & Bar

Map F, P.106

On top of tasty coffee by local roaster Industry Beans, Carolina also serves a delicious array of breakfast classics and hearty light meals with healthy options. Housed in an old shoemaker's shop with its old glass signage retained, the rustic interiors are complemented by a beautiful leafy courtyard – an idyllic setting for a lazy afternoon in the sun. Go for the Tofu Sandwich, made of the house-smoked maple tofu with onion jam and dill pickle, or a Lambwich – a six-hour-braised lamb shoulder dish with beetroot relish, feta, fennel, and rocket salad.

🕐 0730–1530 (M-F), 0830– (Sa-Su)
🏠 11 Nicholson St., Brunswick East
📞 +61 (0)425 842 967
🔗 www.carolinabrunswick.com.au
📘 @CarolinaCafeBar
📷 @carolinacafebrunswick

"The light in the intimate courtyard falls beautifully and feels like someone has opened up their backyard to you for brunch."

– Charlie Romeo Brophy

43 Half Moon Café
Map J, P.108

A short trip north of the CBD leads you to Coburg, a multicultural suburb full of weird and wonderful stores, bars, and restaurants. It is also home to a lot of Middle Eastern eateries like Half Moon Café which has earned a cult following with many locals for its delicious falafels made in the Egyptian style – using broad beans instead of chickpeas. The courtyard is a great place to bite into your order and get a sense of the neighbourhood before setting off to immerse yourself in all that it offers.

🕐 0900–1700 daily
🏠 13 Victoria St., Coburg
📞 +61 (0)3 9350 2949
f Half Moon Cafe

"They have the most delicious falafels I've ever eaten – so fluffy and the pickles are amazing. Explore the neighbourhood! Coburg is a cultural wonderland with many cool shops."

– Billie Justice Thomson

44 Estelle

Map M, P.108

A self-professed venue for all occasions, Estelle provides a chic and comfortable setting for memorable dining and wining in the tree-lined suburb that is Northcote. With its exposed brick walls, recycled timber finish, and tall windows that flood the verdant eating and drinking spaces with light, the restaurant's simple but sophisticated interiors let the contemporary flavours of owner-chef Scott Pickett (and the wines) speak for themselves. Its seasonal Sunday roasts are also worth making time for, so check online to see if one aligns with your visit.

🕐 1230–1600, 1800 till late (F-Su),
1800–2200 (M-Th)
🏠 243–245 High St., Northcote
☎ +61 (0)3 9489 4609
URL www.theestelle.com.au
f @estellebistro
🟐 @estellenorthcote

"A long-time dinner favourite of ours. You can't go wrong with Scott Pickett's cooking (and wine to match)."

– Dom Bartolo & Ryan Guppy, 21-19

 45 Monk Bodhi Dharma
Map S, P.109

Tucked away behind Carlisle Street, Monk Bodhi Dharma may look unassuming from the outside, but upon stepping in, an unexpected world awaits. Besides being a specialist coffee roastery, it also offers an extensive selection of healthy all-day breakfast options through creative re-interpretations of classic dishes. Its house-made bircher muesli, Avignon apple pancakes with dehydrated apple chips, and zucchini hotcakes with beetroot relish are crowd favourites. For dinner, its unique vegan/ gluten-free degustation menus are a must-try. Book your spot on its website beforehand.

🕐 0700–1700 (M–F), 0800– (Sa–Su)
🏠 Rear 202 Carlisle St., Balaclava
📞 +61 (0)3 9534 7250
URL www.monkbodhidharma.com
f @monkbodhidharma

"This hidden gem's house roasted coffee is undeniably the best in Melbourne."

– Glenn Thomas aka The Fox And King

46 Auction Rooms
Map E, P.106

Auction Rooms sits conveniently in the heart of North Melbourne, a gentrified neighbourhood that still brims with old-world charm. Housed in the former WB Ellis Auction House, it offers a reasonably-priced and creative brunch menu which it has become renowned amongst locals for. The coffee is a must-have, where specialty blends are roasted on-site using equipment that complement its chic industrial interiors. Take your pick from its wide selection of beans that you can gift or brew at home.

🕐 0700–1700 (M–F), 0730– (Sa–Su)
🏠 103–107 Errol St., North Melbourne
📞 +61 (0)3 9326 7749
URL www.auctionroomscafe.com.au
f @auctionroomsnorthmelbourne
📷 @auction_rooms

"Make sure you go for a stroll around the backstreets of North Melbourne to check out some of the old heritage buildings."

– Jack Vanzet

 47 **Cumulus Up**
Map B, P.105

Cocooned within a city loft like its namesake, Cumulus Up is a bar that complements its extensive and eclectic selection of wines – housed on-site in its climate-controlled cellar – with a changing flavourful food menu designed by Andrew McConnell and Sam Cheetham. Popular amongst the after-work crowd, its stylish but warm and welcoming interiors feature wooden parquet floors, blown-glass pendant lights, marble tables, steel features, and exposed brickwork that blend harmoniously together to create the perfect setting for intimate dinner and drinks.

🕐 *1700 till late (Tu-Th), 1600 till late (F-Sa)*
🏠 *45 Flinders Ln., CBD* 📞 *+61 (0)3 9654 9545*
🔳 *cumulusup.com.au* 📷 *@cumulusup*

"*The food and drinks are of an exceptional quality that foodies will love. If the duck waffles with foie gras are on the menu, it's a must try.*"

– Alex & Tim Britten-Finschi, FROM BRITTEN P/L

48 Supernormal
Map B, P.105

Supernormal is an Asian-influenced canteen on Flinders Lane with a stylish but understated fit-out that feels Japanese with its open kitchen, countertop dining, vending machines, and karaoke room. Its creative menu will take you on a gastronomic journey through the region through the ingredient choices and dishes influenced by Chinese, Korean, Thai, and Japanese flavours. Wash it all down with the crafted cocktails, or save some room for dessert.

🕐 1100 till late daily
🏠 180 Flinders Ln., CBD
📞 +61 (0)3 9650 8688
🔗 supernormal.net.au
📷 @supernormal_180
🔗 Reservations recommended. Book via website.

"The lobster rolls! Bookings are essential or turn up early."

– Fabio Ongarato, Fabio Ongarato Design

083

Nightlife

Vibrant rooftop bars, live music venues, and open-air screenings

Night owls will never go bored in Melbourne, where countless bars, pubs, and clubs are spread throughout its rooftops, laneways, streets, and suburbs. Like everything else the city offers, there is something for everyone. Places like Chapel Street are a perfect example of its vibrant and diverse nightlife, where you can grab drinks at cosy bars like La La Land (*www.lalaland.com.au*), Wonderland (*www.wonderlandbar.com.au*), or Hoo Ha (*www.hoohaa.com.au*) before dancing the night away at Revolver Upstairs (*revolverupstairs.com.au*) to one of the many big-name DJs who frequently play there. St Kilda is nearby, where you can grab a bite at one of the many eateries along Fitzroy and Acland Streets before heading to the Espy (*The Esplanade Hotel; hotelesplanade.com.au*) if live music is more of your thing. You could also go across the river into the CBD for drinks at Cookie (*www.cookie.net.au*), which is below The Toff in Town (#60) and the Rooftop Bar and Cinema (#22) on Swanston Street. Not far from the CBD is the bustling suburb of Fitzroy, where you can take in the sunset from the Naked in the Sky rooftop bar (*www.nakedforsatan.com.au/in-the-sky*) and catch a gig at The Tote (#58). Other live venue options can be found along Brunswick's Sydney Road and Northcote's High Street. Rather than travel to different suburbs in the course of a night, pick an area and bar hop to avoid spending your time (and $$$) in taxis or trams.

Georgia Perry
Graphic artist

I work with clients from around the world on illustration, graphic design, and fine art projects, as well as produce my own range of products.

Bomba
P.089

Jesse Gerner
Executive chef

I am the executive chef and owner of three Melbourne venues – Añada, Bomba, and Green Park Dining. I live in Thornbury with my wife Vanessa and our three sons.

Kristoffer Paulsen
Photographer & musician

I am a freelance photographer and musician originally from Sydney, but moved to Melbourne in 2007.

Neapoli
Wine Bar
P.088

Le Bon Ton
P.090

David Flack
Founder, Flack Studio

I am an interior architect and designer. I am always excited to discover new treasures, whether on little jaunts around our beautiful city or on regular overseas travels.

Island
Somewhere
P.093

Darcy Prendergast
Founder, Oh Yeah Wow

Darcy Prendergast is an avid fan of dinosaurs, Vikings, and trampolines but also dabbles in the writing and directing of music videos, short films, and TV.

Callan Woolcock
ECD, Jumbla

Jumbla is a motion graphics and animation studio that houses an organised chaos of creators, illusionists, trailblazers, and noise-makers that create award-winning work for a massive variety of clients.

Neighbour-
hood Wine
P.092

Sun Theatre
Yarraville
P.094

Confetti Studio
Design studio

We are Tom Shanahan and Kevin McDowell and we head the multidisciplinary design studio, Confetti. Together we are also one half of wonky hypno-disco band, Mildlife.

Auver Austria
Creative director, AÄRK Collective

AÄRK Collective creates unisex timepieces that are inspired by an appreciation for geometric forms, graphic elements, and timeless design.

Travis Aulsebrook
Musician

Travis Aulsebrook aka Hudson & Troop is a future-folk musician living in the Brunswick East suburb. He has released two EP's and a string of singles, including *The Dream* in 2015.

Tajette O'Halloran
Photographer

I am constantly finding my way and exploring new ideas in photography. I am drawn to the discomposed human ex-perience where I am often the subject of my own work.

Ben Thomas
Photographer & visual artist

I am a photographer, author, brewer, and public Wi-Fi and smart city geek based in Melbourne. I have recently released my first book, *Tiny Tokyo: The Big City Made Mini*.

Chela
Musician & producer

I am Chelsea May, a musician/producer/performer/artist/film-maker. As Chela, I have released singles including *Romanticise* and *Zero* on Kitsune in Paris, and *Handful of Gold* on iHeartComix in LA.

49 Neapoli Wine Bar
Map B, P.104

Neapoli Wine Bar is a sleek space that emits a strong masculine vibe. Its interior is decked out in amber wood, polished concrete, and stainless steel, complementing the wrought iron staircase that takes patrons up to the American oak-lined mezzanine level. Offering the perfect backdrop for cosy conversations, its extensive menu is filled with a scrumptious mix of comfort food and sharing platters that were designed to be washed down by one of the many tasty wines from the cellar.

🕐 *0730 till late (M–F), 0800 till late (Sa)*
🏠 *30 Russell Place, CBD*
📞 *+61 (0)3 9650 5020*
🔗 *www.neapoliwinebar.com.au*
📘 📷 *@NeapoliWineBar*

"*Beautiful fit-out, great service, and delicious food and drinks! It's the perfect place for a Friday knock-off drink (or three).*"

– Georgia Perry

50 Bomba
Map B, P.105

Although there are many rooftop bars in Melbourne, Bomba is extra special. Inspired by the modern bodega, its fit out and ambience are cosy and intimate – different to what one would expect from a similar establishment. Coupled with its red backdrop and woven straw light shades, the nightview of the city skyline is enhanced at the venue. Be sure to try many treats from the tapas menu, which is inspired by the chefs' Spanish roots. Its killer cocktails are also an absolute must-try.

🕒 1500 till late daily
🏠 103 Lonsdale St., CBD
📞 +61 (0)3 9650 5778
🔗 bombabar.com.au
📘📷 @bombabar

"Melburnians particularly love rooftop spaces!"
– Jesse Gerner, Añada, Bomba & Green Park Dining

 51 Le Bon Ton
Map A, P.103

Le Bon Ton is a late-night hangout and supper club tucked away in Collingwood. The Southern American smokehouse, absinthe salon, and cocktail bar is a tribute to the Big Easy and is based around New Orleans' culture, music, and food. Le Bon Ton's relaxed atmosphere makes it the ideal place to chill out after a night out or fuel up before one. Be sure to sample a shot from its wide range of absinthe (if you have yet to try the drink) or tuck into delicious smoked meats that will transport you to another place.

🕐 *Bar: 1200 till late [Restaurant: 1700–2200 (M), 1200–2200 (Tu-Th, Su), –2300 (F-Sa)]*
🏠 51 Gipps St., Collingwood
📞 +61 (0)3 9416 4341
🌐 www.lebonton.com.au
📘 📷 @lebontonmelb

"A wild Louisiana-style saloon serving up cocktails, chilli cheese fries that are addictive, smoked meats, and rocking out till 6am."

– Kristoffer Paulsen

 Neighbourhood Wine
Map F, P.106

Neighbourhood Wine serves seasonal and rustic French-inspired food coupled with wines from every corner of the world. The bistro's candle-lit ambience – coupled with its 1960s and 1970s blues and jazz records that play on high rotation – make it the ideal destination for a romantic rendezvous. Its fascinating back story as an illegal casino and hangout for the Melburnian underworld in the late-1980s also adds to its allure. Although a police raid shut it down 25 years before it was discovered and rejuvenated by its current owner, a lot of its original decor remains untouched.

🕐 1200–0000 (Tu–Su)
🏠 1 Reid St., Fitzroy North
📞 +61 (0)3 9486 8306
🔗 neighbourhoodwine.com
📘📷 @neighbourhoodwine

"Stay late after dinner, have a game of billiards in the Sunset Club, then ask your waiter to show you the secret compartment."

– David Flack, Flack Studio

53 Island Somewhere

Map B, P.104

If you enjoy your drinks with slightly less rambunctious activities on the side, Island Somewhere is the perfect place for you to indulge in a fun and relaxing night out with friends and family. Besides a variety of craft beers and delicious cocktails, it also offers endless entertainment in the form of board games and pinball – the latter playable in a secret location that you have to ask about or stumble across. Rather than dance the night away, test your dexterity on the machines or tickle your mind with rounds of Cluedo, Risk, or Catan. The quirky decor and friendly service staff also make the laidback venue worth the visit.

🕐 1600-0000 (W-Sa)
🏠 213 Franklin St., CBD
📞 +61 (0)3 9326 8324
URL islandsomewhere.business.site
f Island Somewhere

"The main pinball room is somewhat 'hidden' so you might have to ask the bar staff for a clue."

– Darcy Prendergast, Oh Yeah Wow

54 Sun Theatre Yarraville
Map L, P.108

Opened in 1938, Sun Theatre Yarraville has undergone many transformations to become the community institution that it is today. Showing everything from blockbusters to art house specials, its eight boutique cinemas are a film buff-favourite. Besides being a location for The Dressmaker starring Kate Winslet, it even received a surprise visit by Quentin Tarantino and Samuel L. Jackson due to the fact that it attempted to secure a proper 70mm projector to screen their movie, The Hateful 8.

🕐 Check online for programme info
🏠 8 Ballarat St., Yarraville
📞 +61 (0)3 9362 0999
URL suntheatre.com.au
f @suntheatreyarraville

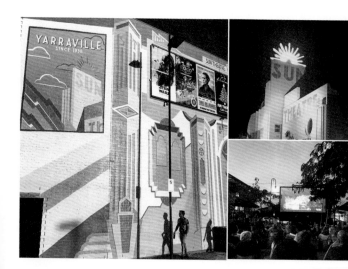

"Great place to watch the latest movies, the classics, and of course, the festivals too."

– Callan Woolcock, Jumbla

55 Hugs & Kisses
Map B, P.104

Hugs and Kisses is a members-only club that knows how to throw a good party. Its decks are often (wo-)manned by some of Melbourne's best underground DJs, while its stage frequently features a talented band performing live. The club's interiors could be best described as 'decadent with an affinity for the absurd'. Its owners are currently on the hunt for a new location, so be sure to check online for updates. To become a member before a party, simply fill out a form on the website.

URL hugsandkisses.club
f @hugsandkissesclub
⌀ Membership Registration: hugsandkisses.club/new-member

"Newcomers are welcomed with open arms. Just be sure to sign up on their website. Stay hydrated."
– Tom Shanahan & Kevin McDowell, Confetti Studio

 56 LongPlay
Map F, P.106

LongPlay is a low-key bar set amid a converted shopfront with a private cinema space that provides a contrasting experience to that of traditional cinema houses. Its warm and welcoming interiors feature a stylish mix of Danish furnishings; blending the settings of an American diner and an old Italian bistro. Besides its delicious Mediterranean-inspired share-plates, LongPlay is also known for its exceptional classic and contemporary cocktails that will not cost you a fortune either.

🕐 1800–2300 (Su–W), –0100 (Th–Sa)
🏠 318 St Georges Rd., Northcote
📞 +61 (0)423 115 774 URL www.longplay.net.au
f LongPlay 🖉 Reservations recommended. Book via website.

"Organise a screening of a movie of your choice with friends (maximum 30 people). It's an intimate and memorable way to watch a film together."

– Auver Austria, AĀRK Collective

57 Some Velvet Morning
Map Q, P.109

Some Velvet Morning is one of Melbourne's smallest live music venues but what it lacks in size, it makes up for in entertainment. With a name that was taken from a famous Nancy Sinatra and Lee Hazelwood duet, the bar books some of the best acts in Melbourne and beyond, which play several nights a week. Its intimate backroom space is fitted out like a cosy living room, and it serves Athenian street food prepared by Greek restaurant Triakosia .

🕐 1600-2300 (Tu-W), -0100 (Th-Sa), -2200 (Su)
🏠 123 Queens Parade, Clifton Hill
📞 +61 (0)3 5928 9714
🔗 somevelvetmorning.com.au
📷 @somevelvetmorning123
🔗 Check online for programme info.

"Owned by musicians and the friendliest bunch of people, this place books the best local music. Try the nachos, they're top notch."

– Travis Aulsebrook aka Hudson & Troop

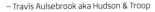

 58 The Tote
Map A, P.103

The Tote is one of Melbourne's favourite live rock-and-roll venues; an institution so loved that 20,000 people marched in protest to save it from closure in 2010. Upon the march's success, the strict licensing laws that threatened many venues like The Tote were changed. Its band room is often packed when gigs are on, which is most nights, so be sure to arrive early to secure your spot. There is also a large outdoor courtyard where you can catch your breath after all the dancing, and if you want to listen to any of your favourite songs, take control of the jukebox at the front bar.

🕐 1600-0100 (W), -0300 (Th-Sa), -2300 (Su)
🏠 67-71 Johnston St., Collingwood
📞 +61 (0)3 9419 5320 🔗 thetotehotel.com
📘📷 @thetotehotel 🔗 Check online for programme info.

"Yay! It's dirty. It's loud. The carpet is sticky as hell but there's no other place like it. Drink responsibly."

– Tajette O'Halloran

59 Horse Bazaar
Map B, P.104

Neatly tucked away in Melbourne's CBD is Horse Bazaar, a Japanese-influenced restaurant and bar that fuses visual arts with live music, speciality drinks, and izakaya-inspired soul food. The venue has long been a hub for creative minds and the digital arts scene, as seen via its 20-metre long canvas where new media and digital artwork are projected on most nights. Its extensive bottled beer menu offers a wide variety of brews from all over the world, and its crafted cocktails are a must-try.

🕐 1700 till late (M-Th, Sa), 1200 till late (F)
🏠 397 Little Lonsdale St., CBD
📞 +61 (0)3 9670 2329
🌐 www.horsebazaar.com.au
📘 @HorseBazaarMelb 📷 @horsebazaar
🔗 Check online for programme info.

"There's a showcase of some of the best hip hop and beats to be found in Melbourne, teamed up with the craziest projection setups I've seen."

– Ben Thomas

60 The Toff in Town
Map B, P.104

The Toff in Town is an iconic Melbourne venue that hosts some of Melbourne (and beyond)'s greatest musical artists and comedians. It is split into several sections that include the stage side and the main dining or drinking area, which is dominated by train carriage-like booths that allow for cosy conversations. If you manage to snag one of these coveted spots, ring for service to order your food or cocktails. There are also two outdoor areas to hang out in if you need some fresh air.

🕐 1700 till late daily   🏠 Level 2, Curtin House.,
252 Swanston St., CBD   📞 +61 (0)3 9639 8770
🔲 www.thetoffintown.com
📘📷 @thetoffintown
🔗 Check online for programme info.

"Look up the band room schedule online so you can head there on a night in which you can discover one of your new favourite bands."
– Chela

DISTRICT MAP : **CARLTON, FITZROY**

MAP A

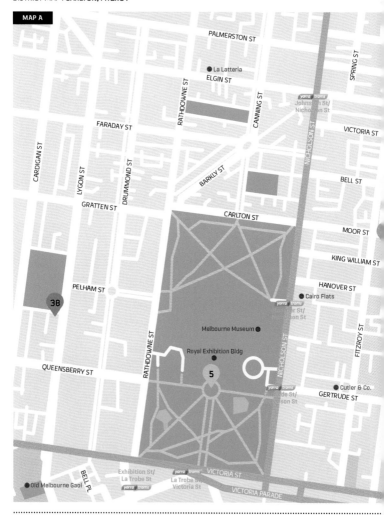

- 5_Carlton Gardens & Royal Exhibition Building
- 17_Daine Singer
- 38_Parco Canteen
- 41_Grub Fitzroy

MAP B

- 6_Manchester Unity Building
- 10_Nicholas Building
- 21_Bird's Basement
- 22_Rooftop Cinema
- 33_Dinosaur Designs
- 34_Wunderkammer
- 49_Neapoli Wine Bar
- 53_Island Somewhere
- 55_Hugs & Kisses
- 59_Horse Bazaar
- 60_The Toff in Town

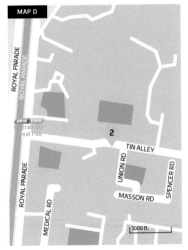

- 2_University of Melbourne
- 3_Federation Square
- 4_Melbourne Cricket Ground
- 7_Forum Melbourne
- 18_Craft Victoria
- 32_Lucy Folk
- 47_Cumulus Up
- 48_Supernormal
- 50_Bomba

DISTRICT MAPS : **NORTH MELBOURNE, BRUNSWICK EAST, FITZROY NORTH**

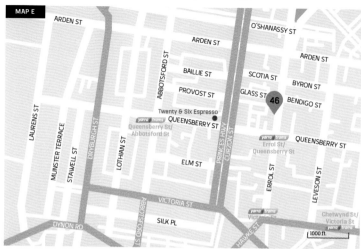

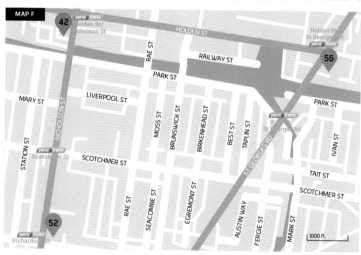

- ● 42_Carolina Café & Bar
- ● 46_Auction Rooms
- ● 52_Neighbourhood Wine
- ● 56_LongPlay

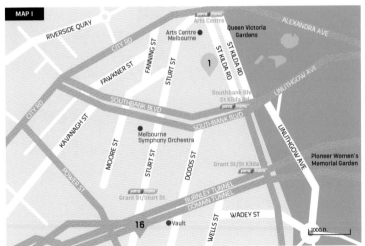

- 1_NGV International
- 15_Robin Boyd Foundation
- 16_ACCA
- 27_Dixons Recycled Records

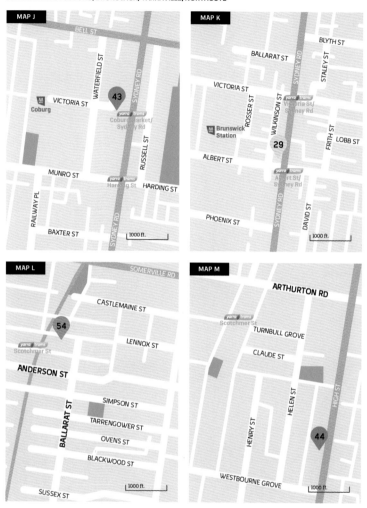

- 29_Mr Kitly
- 43_Half Moon Café
- 44_Estelle
- 54_Sun Yarraville

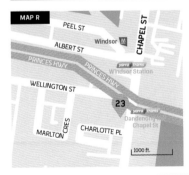

- 8_Abbotsford Convent
- 23_The Astor Theatre
- 24_St Kilda Twilight Market
- 39_SUPERRANDOM
- 45_Monk Bodhi Dharma
- 57_Some Velvet Morning

DISTRICT MAPS : **DOCKLANDS, ST ANDREWS, BULLEEN, KEW, CAMBERWELL, GEMBROOK**

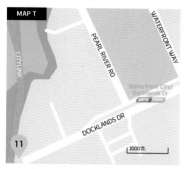

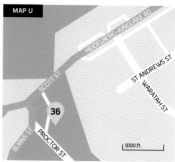

- 11_Moonee Ponds Creek Trail
- 13_Heide Museum of Modern Art
- 14_Lyon Housemuseum
- 35_Camberwell Sunday Market
- 36_St Andrews Market
- 37_The Independent

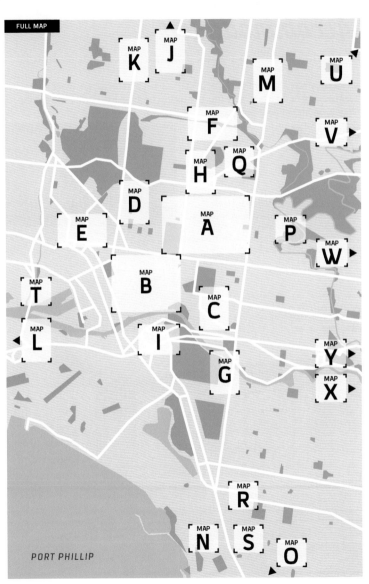

PORT PHILLIP

Accommodation

Hip hostels, fully-equipped apartments & swanky hotels

No journey is perfect without a good night's sleep to recharge. Whether you're backpacking or on a business trip, our picks combine top quality and convenience, whatever your budget.

 < $150    $151–250 $251+

Adelphi Hotel

As Melbourne's first verified design hotel, Adelphi combines stellar service, a convenient location, and an intimate setting with quirky decorative touches. Its unique dessert-themed interiors are elegant and understated; perfectly complementing its iconic cantilevered rooftop pool that overlooks Flinders Lane.

🏠 *187 Flinders Ln., CBD*
📞 *+61 (0)3 8080 8888*
URL *adelphi.com.au*

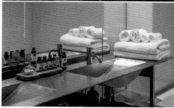

Coppersmith

A stone's throw away from Albert Park Lake and the Melbourne Sports & Aquatic Centre lies Coppersmith, a boutique hotel with a bistro, bar, and rooftop retreat. Housing only a limited number of guestrooms, it guarantees privacy and personalisation for a memorable stay.

🏠 *435 Clarendon St., South Melbourne*
📞 *+61 (0)3 8696 7777*
🌐 *coppersmithhotel.com.au*

Crown Metropol

🏠 *8 Whiteman St., Southbank*
📞 *+61 (0)3 9292 8888*
🔗 *www.crownhotels.com.au*

The Prince

🏠 *2 Acland St., St Kilda*
📞 *+61 (0)3 9536 1111*
🔗 *theprince.com.au*

Hotel Lindrum Melbourne

🏠 26 Flinders St., CBD
📞 +61 (0)3 9668 1111
URL www.hotellindrum.com.au

Middle Park Hotel

🏠 102 Canterbury Rd., Middle Park
📞 +61 (0)3 9810 0079
URL middleparkhotel.com.au

NOTEL

🏠 388 Flinders Lane
📞 +61 428 952 559
URL notelmelbourne.com.au

Notes

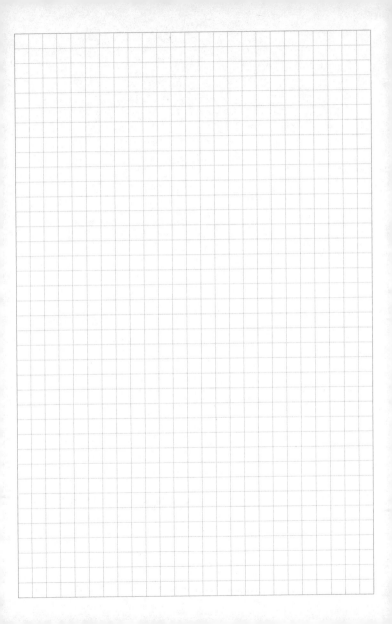

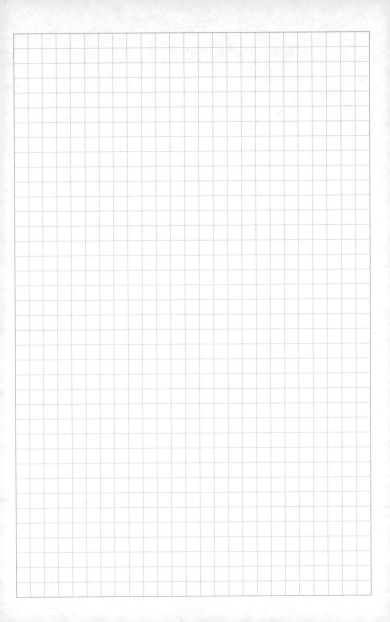

Index

CITIX60

CITIx60: Melbourne

Published and distributed by
viction workshop ltd

viction:ary™

7C Seabright Plaza, 9-23 Shell Street,
North Point, Hong Kong

Url: www.victionary.com
Email: we@victionary.com
🗗 www.facebook.com/victionworkshop
🐦 www.twitter.com/victionary_
📷 @victionworkshop

Edited and produced by viction:ary

Concept & art direction: Victor Cheung
Research & editorial: Queenie Ho, Caroline Kong
Project coordination: Jovan Lip, Katherine Wong
Design & map illustration: Frank Lo, MW Wong, Scarlet Ng

Contributing writer: Trent Carslake
Cover map illustration: Ellen Porteus
Count to 10 illustrations: Guillaume Kashima aka Funny Fun
Photography: Daniel Aulsebrook

Content is compiled based on facts available as of July 2019. Travellers are
advised to check for updates from respective locations before your visit.

First edition
ISBN 978-988-79726-5-5
Printed and bound in China

Acknowledgements

A special thank you to all creatives, photographers, editors, producers, companies, and organisations for your crucial contributions to our inspiration and
knowledge necessary for the creation of this book. And, to the many whose
names are not credited but have participated in the completion of the book,
we thank you for your input and continuous support.

CITIX60
City Guides

CITIx60 is a handpicked list of hotspots that illustrates the spirit of the world's most exhilarating design hubs. From what you see to where you stay, this city guide series leads you to experience the best — the places that only passionate insiders know and go.

Each volume is a unique collaboration with local creatives from selected cities. Known for their accomplishments in fields as varied as advertising, architecture, graphics, fashion, industrial design, food, music, and publishing, they are at the cutting edge of what's on and when. Whether it's a one-day stopover or a longer trip, **CITIx60** is your inspirational guide.

Stay tuned for new editions.

City guides available now:

Amsterdam
Barcelona
Berlin
Copenhagen
Hong Kong
Istanbul
Lisbon
London
Los Angeles
Melbourne
Milan
New York
Paris

Portland
San Francisco
Singapore
Stockholm
Taipei
Tokyo
Vancouver
Vienna